EXAMINATION OF AZ91E WITH NI 0.21 CA 0.03

ANIL KUMAR MATTA

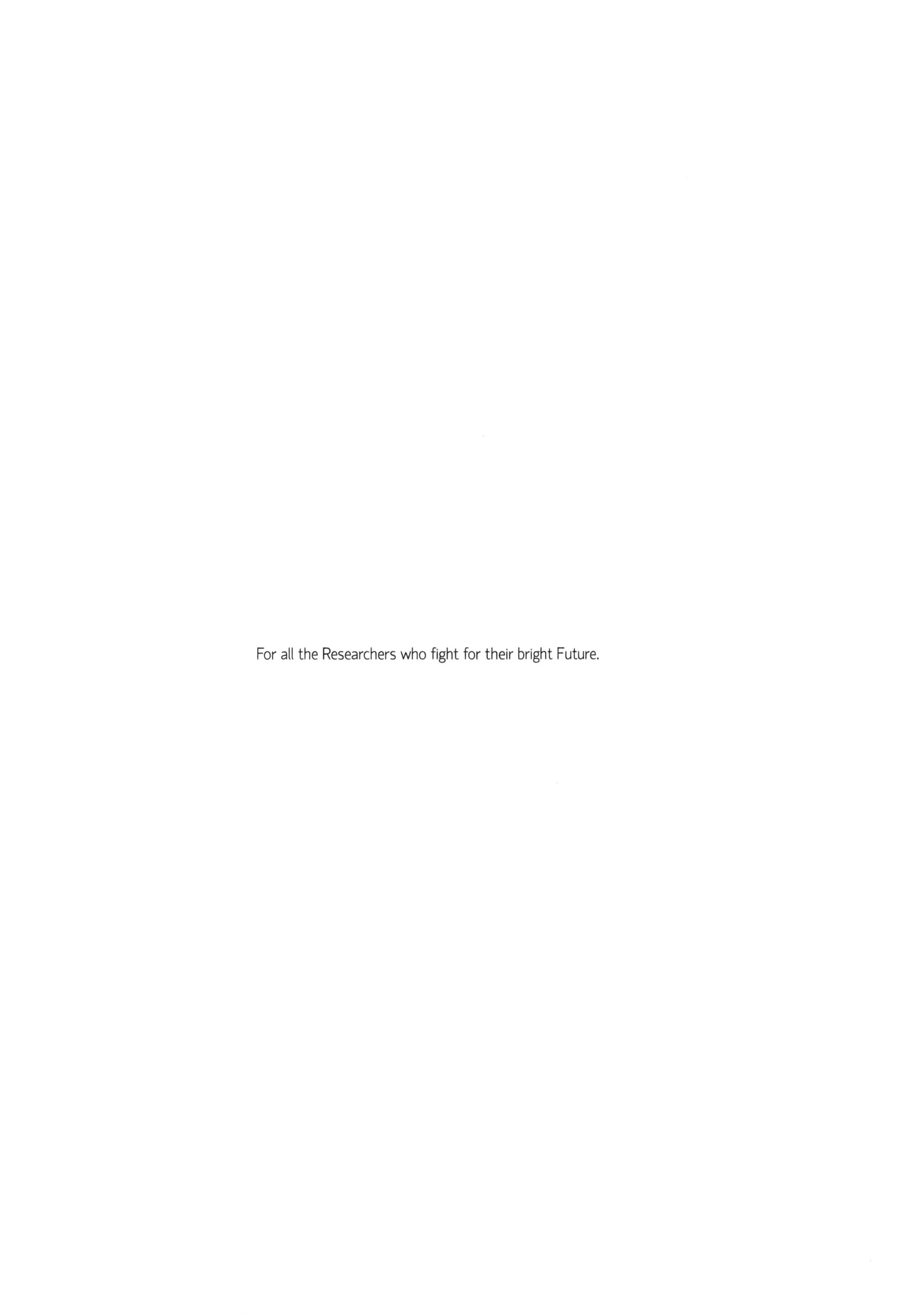

For all the Researchers who fight for their bright Future.

Contents

Foreword

This work is brought into market with a strong zeal to help Fresh scientists, Engineers, Researchers and Future Aspirants. A thorough examination of AZ91E with 0.21 Ni 0.03 Ca is done with care. The materials software Thermocalc is used to examine the composition.

This examination is done with a vision to develop new AZE Series.

Anil Kumar Matta

CEO- Natas Consultancy

Preface

THERMOCALC is a versatile program capable of calculating conventional phase diagrams, petro genetic grids, and pseudo sections. THERMOCALC contains two main components: the application itself, and the internally consistent thermodynamic dataset it uses. Solution models are continually added to the thermodynamic dataset enabling modeling to more precisely approximate natural systems.

THERMOCALC requires three input files in order to operate: a preference file, a file containing the thermodynamic properties of the phases, and a file that contains coded a-X (activity-composition)relationships of the solid solution phases as well as scripts to specify the type of calculation to perform and the rock composition. Choosing the correct chemical system is vital for representing the compositions of all the phases in interest. The chemical system K_2O-FeO-MgO-Al_2O_3-SiO_2-H_2O (KFMASH) has been very successful in modeling reactions.

Anil Kumar Matta

CEO- Natas Consultancy

Acknowledgements

On the family front, I was honored to have a strong family and particularly my better half Smitha & Dhanvi who has taken extra weights for my purpose to manage different familial errands, broadening her full help and enabling me to concentrate on the profession.

I am obligated to my parents, my brothers and in-laws for affecting my manner of thinking and for their broadened bolster all through my scholastic undertakings. My father Matta Kishore Kumar (retired Station Superintendent, South Central Railway, India) had relentlessly guided me as a father, friend, advisor, mentor and as a personal coach. He would bestow his blessings always on me.

And, I take pride in devoting the present my consultancy work to my cherished guardians who had relinquished their solaces and attempted to raise every last one of our relatives. They had inserted us with basic reasoning and center moral esteems and helped us to develop as model subjects and great individuals. Particularly my parents had offered me every opportunity to grow and succeed in my life.

Thank You all,
Matta Anil Kumar
CEO-Natas Consultancy
Natas Consultancy, Natas Heights, Vijayawada, AP, India -520011
Email: anilkumarmatta7@gmail.com, anilnatas@natasconsultancy.co.in
Ph: (+91)9652842089/ 8096558651
https://rapid-prototyping-consultancy.business.site

Prologue

ZE41A is the most commercially sand cast magnesium alloy in the industry. The major disadvantage of this alloy is its very poorer corrosion resistance as compared to AZ91E, WE43A & EV31A. However, it should be finely noted that the minimum yield strength (Mechanical Property) of specimen cut from ZE41A is higher than the ultimate tensile strength (Mechanical Property) of those for AZ91E.

CHAPTER ONE

Software Based Examination

This chapter is the extension of the Book 'Making of AZ91E Series' Notion Press, where clear cut picture is given to select the compositions with elements based on requirements. In this chapter a complete examination is focused on AZ91E with Ni 21% and Ca 3%.

1.1 Material

The material AZ91E along with Ni 21% Ca 3% is taken for investigation. The complete composition of AZ91E is shown in Fig.1.1. Therefore the new investigation composition is Al (8.84)Zn(0.61)Mn(0.18)Fe(0.02)Si(0.02)Cu(0.005)Zr(0.002)Ni(0.21)Ca(0.03)Mg(90.083).

1.2 Property Models

Based on the free version of software Ni(0.21)Ca(0.03)Mg(99.76) compositions are investigated. Fig.1.2. Shows Ni 0.21Ca 0.03Mg 99.76 Hot Cracking Susceptibility.

A phase diagram showing spinodal curves, with in the binodal coexistence outers and the two critical points: one upper and the lower critical solution temperature gives spinodal temperature i.e outer periphery temperature Fig.1.3.

T zero temperature is the absolute zero at which a thermodynamic system will have lowest energy. It is -273.15 °C on Celsius and -459.67 °F on the Fahrenheit for Ni 0.21Ca 0.03Mg 99.76 it is at 655°C and 847°C shown in Fig.1.4.

Investigation of Property models are shown in Fig.1.2 to 1.4.

1.3 Thermo Calc [1] [2] Fig.1.5 to 1.13

From the software investigations Mole fraction and mass fraction are obtained as shown in Fig.1.5. From Fig.1.6 The step in temperature for the composition is exactly at 923 K. From Software results 1.7, 1.8 it is clearly evident that the presence of HCP structure gives more strength to the new series alloy. Investigations of 1.9 a & b shows 0.8 mole fraction of solid at 650⁰c (as the slope of lines vary) by Scheil and Equilibrium Solidification.

Al	Zn	Mn	Fe	Si	Cu	Zr	Mg
8.84	0.61	0.18	0.02	0.02	0.005	<0.002	Bal.

Fig.1.1: AZ91E Mg. Alloy wt. percent

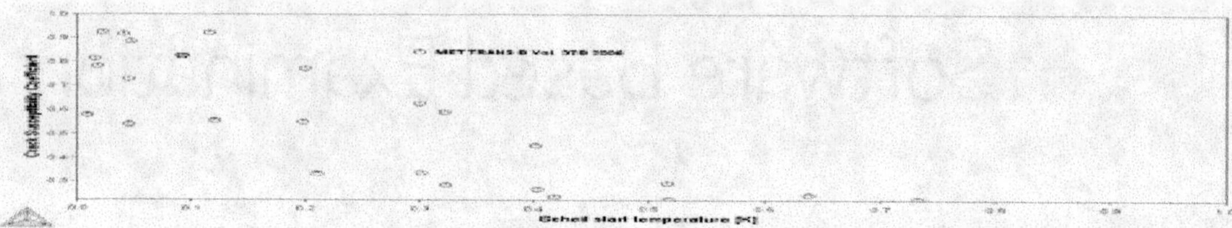

Fig.1.2: Ni 0.21Ca 0.03Mg 99.76 Hot Cracking Susceptibility

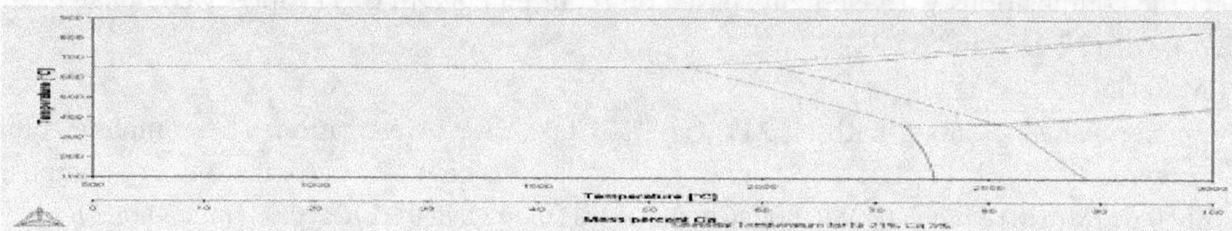

Fig.1.3: Ni 0.21Ca 0.03Mg 99.76 Spinodal Temperature

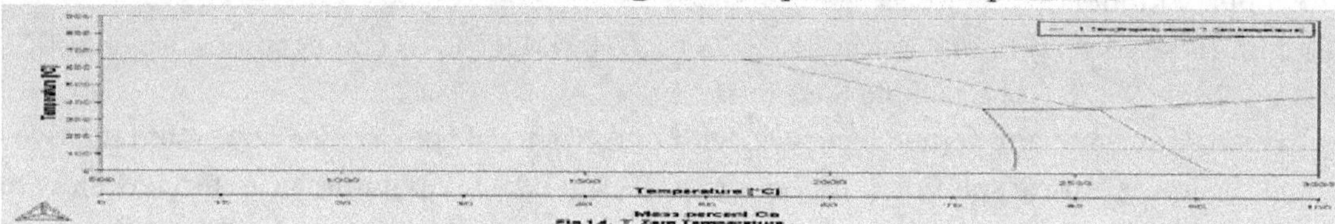

Fig.1.4: Ni 0.21Ca 0.03Mg 99.76 T Zero Temperature

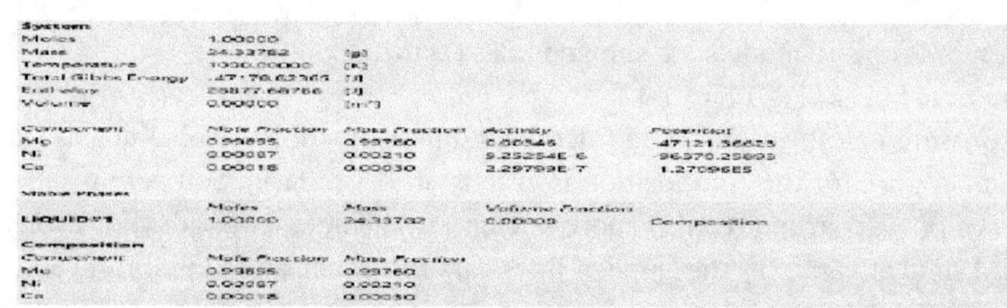

Fig.1.5: Ni 0.21Ca 0.03Mg 99.76 Single Point Equilibrium

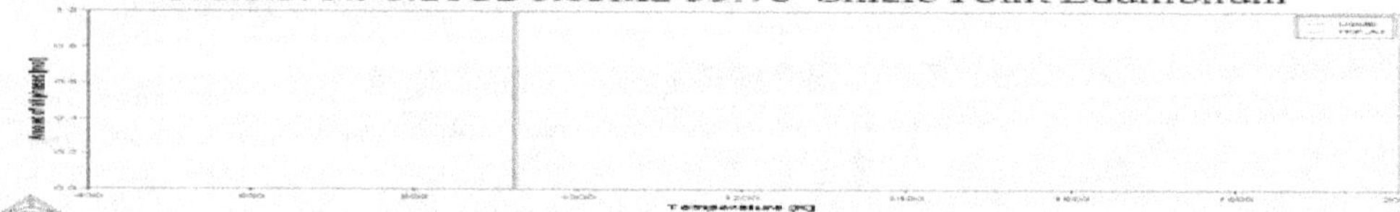

Fig.1.6: Ni 0.21Ca 0.03Mg 99.76 Step in Temperature

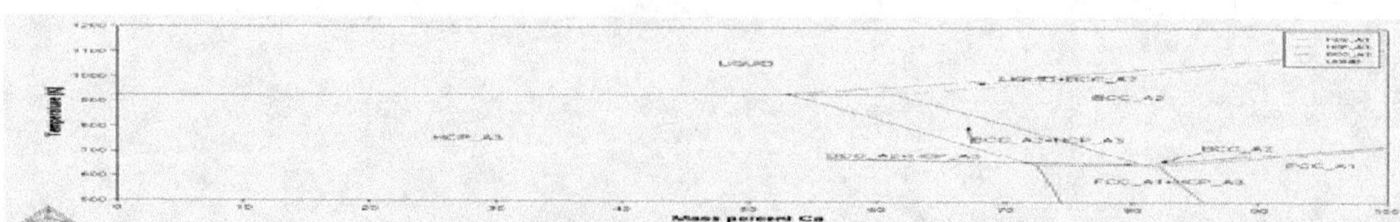

Fig.1.7: Ni 0.21Ca 0.03Mg 99.76 Phase Diagram

Figs: 1.1 to 1.7

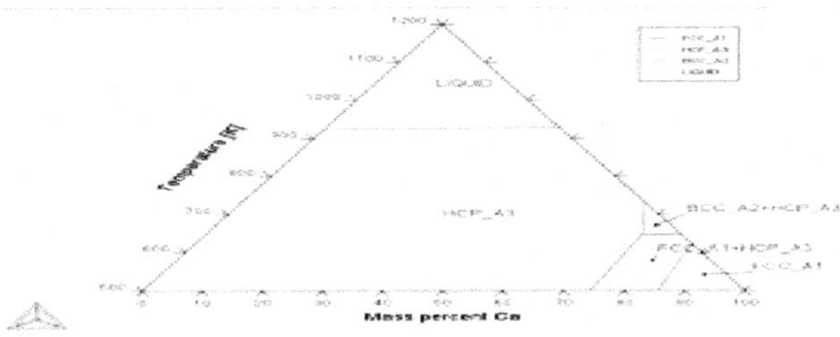

Fig.1.8: Ni 0.21 Ca 0.03 Mg 99.76 Ternary Phase Diagram

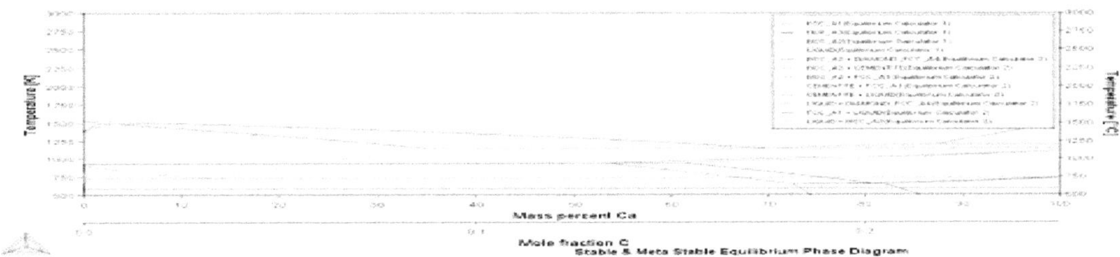

Fig.1.9a: Ni 0.21 Ca 0.03 Mg 99.76 Stable and Meta stable Phase Diagram

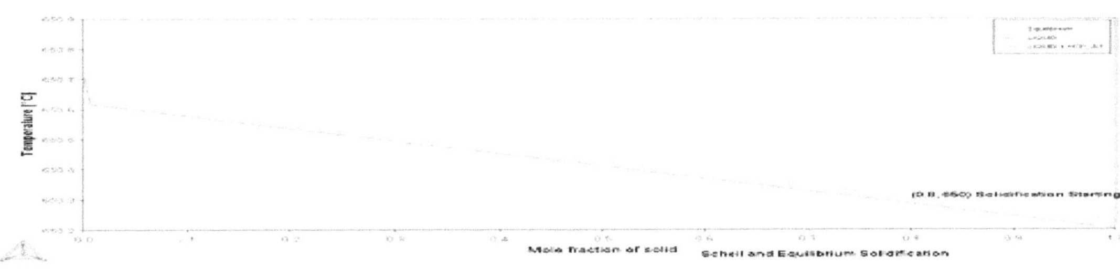

Fig.1.9b: Ni 0.21 Ca 0.03 Mg 99.76 Scheil and Equilibrium Solidification

Mole fraction of solid	Temperature [°C]
0.00000	650.71200
-4.44089E-16	650.71200
-4.44089E-16	650.71200
0.00701	650.61600
0.00701	650.61600
1.00000	650.20200

Fig.1.10: Ni 0.21 Ca 0.03 Mg 99.76 Scheil and Equilibrium Solidification Table renderer

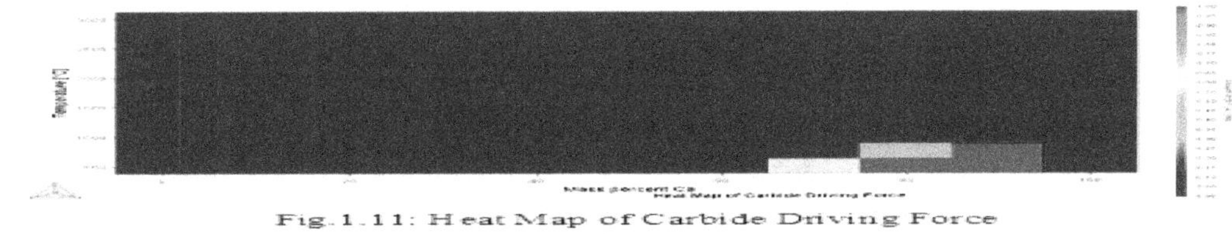

Fig.1.11: Heat Map of Carbide Driving Force

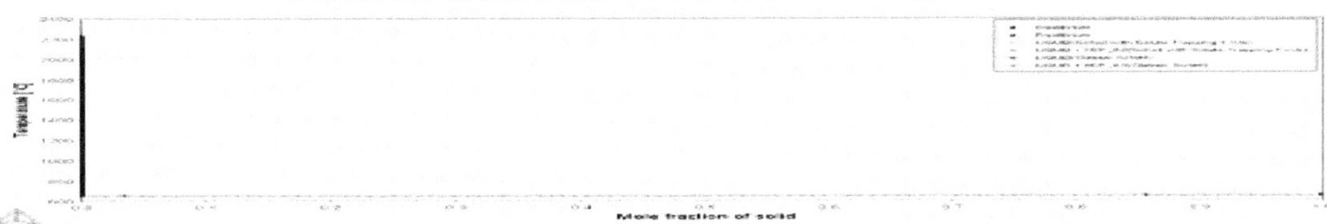

Fig.1.12: Scheil with solute trapping

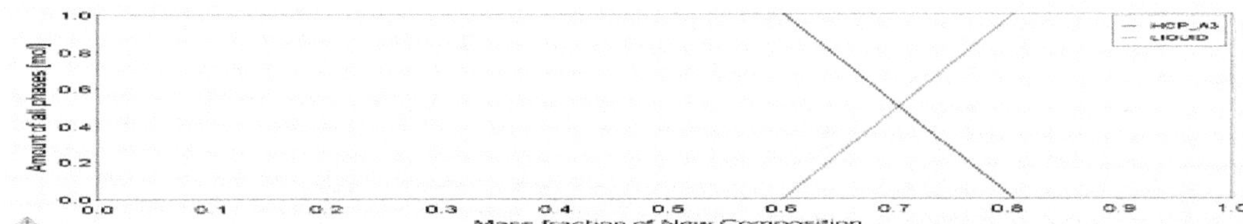

Fig.1.13: Material to Material

Figs: 1.8 to 1.13

CHAPTER TWO

Conclusions

- The new composition AZ91E series with Ni 0.21Ca 0.03Mg 99.76 showed HCP structure which shows huge strength for non ferrous alloy.
- The Solidification rates depicted that alloy is homogeneous and resists light weight.
- From Phase Diagrams we suggest that solid solubility will be with no miscibility gaps.
- Also from various temperature analysis like spinodal, outer surface cracks cannot be formed.
- And finally based on the software examination this Alloy can be prototyped and tested.

CHAPTER THREE

References

1. Anil Kumar Matta. Making of AZ91E Series: Notion Press Publisher Based in India, Chennai. ISBN 9798887176369.
2. Natas Consultancy. https://rapid-prototyping-consultancy.business.site